The Hutton Inquiry

CHRIS MCCABE was born in Liverpool in 1977. He has worked in several jobs since graduating from university, mostly as a side issue to writing poetry. His work has been published in numerous journals, including *Poetry Salzburg Review*, *Angel Exhaust* and *Great Works*. He has also read at the Cambridge Conference of Contemporary Poetry 2004 and in the Crossing the Line Series at the Poetry Café. He currently works as Assistant Librarian at the Poetry Library, London. This is his first book.

The Hutton Inquiry

Chris McCabe

Cambridge

PUBLISHED BY SALT PUBLISHING
PO Box 937, Great Wilbraham, Cambridge PDO CB1 5JX United Kingdom

All rights reserved

© Chris McCabe, 2005

The right of Chris McCabe to be identified as the
author of this work has been asserted by him in accordance
with Section 77 of the Copyright, Designs and Patents Act 1988.

This book is in copyright. Subject to statutory exception
and to provisions of relevant collective licensing agreements,
no reproduction of any part may take place without the written
permission of Salt Publishing.

First published 2005

Printed and bound in the United Kingdom by Lightning Source

Typeset in Swift 9.5 / 13

*This book is sold subject to the conditions that it shall not,
by way of trade or otherwise, be lent, re-sold, hired out,
or otherwise circulated without the publisher's prior consent
in any form of binding or cover other than that in which
it is published and without a similar condition including this
condition being imposed on the subsequent purchaser.*

ISBN 1 84471 074 2 paperback

SP

1 3 5 7 9 8 6 4 2

This book is dedicated to the life and memory of my dad Paul McCabe (1948–2004)

Contents

A TASTE OF VERDIGRIS	1
A Taste of Verdigris	3
Milton Keynes	6
Modern Realist Keep-Fit Poem	7
Twilight Fishing	8
Fancy an Indian	9
Poems for Lunch	10
Michelangelo Manufactured by the Murdoch Empire	12
Père-Lachaise Cemetery	14
Interpreting Flying Dreams	16
A Piglet Imperialism	17
Cititrix	18
Two for the Zoo	19
Flossing for Fishhooks	20
Sky Tree Wank Star	21
Post-Its	22
Network	23
running poet's heart thinks in free verse when it rains	24
Case Study	25
Garbagesleep	26
The Other Tonight	27
Babalaas	29
Dylan's Bust	30
The Garden Party	32
Dance of the Victorian Remote Control	33

PROGRESS POEMS 37
   # 1,502: *letter to rupert murdoch regarding his smile*   39
   # 601: *punk*   40
   # 1,991: *kiss my arse or I'll kick your head in*   41
   # 11: *wittgenstein*   43
   # 1,336: *1938*   44
   # 227: *lunch-break powernap:*   45
   # 902: *graduating*   46
   # 1,927: *annual conference:*   47
   # 1,394: *the allies*   49
   # 743: *thatcher & the brighton bomb*   50
   # 1,492: *tHE sTAND-dOWN cOMEDIAN:*   52
   # 185: *search engines*   53
   # 838: *the class divide*   54
   # 764: *painting the sky:*   55
   #1,291: *beyond iraq*   56
   # 800: *ivor cutler*   57
   # 1,772: *a drunk man compares teenage pregnancies to a horse chestnut*   58
   # 192: *suburbs train*   60
   # 659: *cleaning habits:*   61
   # 255: *darwin*   62
   # 666: *surprise visitations*   64
   # 592: *theatre of war*   65
   # 1,906: *bonnie & clyde*   66
   #374: *revisionist theories*   67
   # 433: *the jogger*   68
   # 171: *mobile phone games in first class*   69
   # 1,333: *defining genre:*   70

# 555: *george w. bush*	71
# 302: *indexing blighty*	72
# 87: *bakhtin's smoking habits*	73
# 21: *the martyrs*	74
# 1,803: *the lads*	75
# 457: *a perfect imagist poem*	76
# 409: *on the night bus:*	77
# 702: *the union*	78
# 959: *television networks*	79
#1,857: *media coverage*	80
# 1,687: *backseat activism*	81
# 328: *management styles:*	82
# 1,531: *internet death of chris mccabe*	83
#278: *genetically modified*	84
# 819: *barflies*	86
# 526: *some propaganda*	87
# 972: *pre-reading reception:*	88
# 189: *vincent van gogh*	89
# 1,111: *ezra pound*	90
# 911: *self-referential poetics*	91
# 1,174: *industrial reminder*	92
# 850: *red label classification in the letter library*	93
# 1,061: *sunday morning*	94
#133: *the office*	95
# 50: *james joyce*	96
# 471: *a particularised history of cocaine*	97
# 1,002: *rome; a play in eleven lines*	98
# 299: *thank you tony*	99
# 1,463: *michael jackson*	100

# 986: *winter*	101
# 1,600: *in england*	102
# 701: *maslow*	103
# 1,094: *billy the kid retires, marries & turns to poetry*	104
# 1,744: *the hippocritopotamus*	105
# 842: *wittgenstein 2*	106
# 1,231: *shopping*	107
# 170: *the divorce rate*	108
# 1,192: *osama bin laden*	110
THE SMOG: LONDON POEMS	111
The London Weather News	113
Untitled	114
Three London Poems	115
Zone	117
Jogging in the Country Park	118
Any Normal Day in Dagenham	119
London Migration Sequence	120
THE HUTTON INQUIRY	127
"22 May — a meeting . . ."	130
"processes of summer . . ."	131
"best game . . ."	132
"one man's notion . . ."	133
"Dr Kelly described . . ."	134
"similarity in appearance . . ."	135
"pre-emptive attack . . ."	136
"Email hours . . ."	137

"washing on the line: in the house style . . ."	138
so every book is a car, then?	140
A New Iraqi Flag	141
A Late Arrival	142
Crikey	143
High-Risk Sunday League Strategy	144
SOME TRINKETS: FOR SARAH	145
Some Trinkets	147
A Note for Sarah	148
Shortwood	149
Slices	151
The Girl Who Cried Fox	153
A Christmas Poem	154
Fairy Tale: The Wolf & the Book	155
Uttoxeter	157
Delicious	159

Acknowledgements

Acknowledgements are due to the editors of the following magazines where these poems, or versions of them, first appeared. Many thanks to all of you: *Angel Exhaust*; *Cambridge Contemporary Conference of Poetry 2004: CCCP14*; *Fire*; *Great Works* (www.greatworks.org); *Keystone*; *Lamport Court*; *Neon Highway*; *Orbis*; *Poetry Salzburg Review*. Thanks also go to Stephen Raw for the cover image.

A Taste of Verdigris

A Taste of Verdigris

PAYDAY

that unmistakable feeling

enchanting

fairytale landscape

masquerading as empire

DELIA

sanitised kitchenry self-embezzled in an honest
understanding of weight issues
the great connexion on the big topic
either up for the butter
or flat out on the fat
unspoilt & still in
partaking at the petit-bourgeois patisserie
amazes this, all from white like doves
the egg's hardboiled & unfreckled
laid in marble
& between the shell & the membrane
a little air pocket
like a navel — or from another perspective —
keegan's chin —
a miracle self-made plexi-pop:

if it floats in water, reject it.

duff air between the shell & membrane:
that my dear is where we reside.

THREE KINDS OF LIES:

    lies

    damn lies

& the core LI£$ we had to learn

    A LITTLE BET

four   for fun
when the going's good
at the tip
of the survival/pleasure paradigm
folded later into £1.28
embarrassment curbed
by a decent bookie
like he wants me to win
"if we owe it, we'll pay it"
exchanged for the four mile round trip
& the week's chopped tomatoes

    EXTENDED OVERDRAFT

the day the overdraft extended
(three years, rejected)
blood watered electric barclaysblue.

strange   this feeling of winning.

    READY, STEADY . . .

citizens: the chizel in the potato jawed presenter
confesses to sex on the dancefloor & an unnatural
attraction to the shortcrust tory chef

before offering today's pearler:
the problem with 2-for-1 offers
is that you buy one & throw one away

apparently

    SOME SAVINGS SET ASIDE

ones & twos crawled like limescale's chainmail
up the 'volvic' bottle
for the totem exchange
of a new set of pans

    TASTE OF THE COLOUR OF MONEY

synaesthesia of the money buffer
copper & the taste of verdigris

Milton Keynes

grey glass pocket shots of Milton Keynes
a language made of oohs & ahs
emotion hits the orange zone   19:45:58
sun salmonpink defied not to retain on the retina
& if so, to burn out the negative with a spotted torch—
happier than ever before is a palpable thing
in the seats in front
bassett's liquorice allsorts & REAL LIFE magazine
reflection in the mirrored cubicle
throws back plasmascreen white
slightly more boozeworn than it was before
though it's a toughy for you   I know
to ask for leave
to hold the hand   the very hand
of the Drinking Machine

Modern Realist Keep-Fit Poem

it Emails itself, this poem: two weeks
before reading—replicated in inbox
incurring an acute sense of déjà vu
on immediate impression—

triangle lionlight scrolled full on her face, smiling—

Re: definitions of culture:
lexical finger-trigger compressed between 'cell-phone'
& the stalling descriptor like lighter flint or scalextrix
sparked plastic at the syllabic bend
ce' ce' ce' ce' ce' ce' ce' ce' ce'
'cellulite' said at last with self-disgust
like its news to us (shakespeare complete CD-Rom: no hits)
tinned meat jelly resealed in sausage skin
ugly: yes, but arseways up in the flood

      in the jacuzzi
buoyant on an airwet jiffy bag
patrol hit the switch which flattens the surface
to check drowned bald prairie of sex
which we foresee & fart mutually
so someone at patrol suggests the switch wasn't pressed
& bubbles sing perineums again

      through the glass
fitness suitors, lycra digital mapped thighs
registers energy burned tracks under trains
sliding safe / less safe / unsafe
punctuated with an introduction to spiritual journeys
lap warmed legroom windscreen visored light
               —radio radio radio
& sweetwrapper full glove compartments

Twilight Fishing
for Ste

1

sparrow's attention span. clockwork birds in the deranged tree.
shards of the glass months shattered over the pond top. heart-thump
of the rod. musclekick in the snot-net. line like light from a nightlamp
lost in the empty eyesocket of the black throat. fleshbone of larynx.
cut it. *let it swim*. red-gold kick. sinking glove. guilt image exact on
the retina smeared to surface. *that will probably die now* I said. I don't
think I thought it would.

2

this was the truth one. *carp*: wood-carved in the mouth. not *a* but *the*
—shock caught watched in the eye of the lake. known silt mover of the
nightdrunk angler. known selfstamped genuine of the book; the first
over europe's jolt roads hybridised to ghost carp offspring. becoming
still under wet paper's see-through skin   soft-ripped. cool release in black
monastery pools—memories, matins, bells—submerged heartleaves of fins.
dissolving in twilight before the too-late. to mooncap its vision & try to
lift its weight. to try to. to hold up gold.

Fancy an Indian

Canadian mountains
in summer
glib blue
in the booth
kitsch
with a quote
unrelatable
"out out brief candle
life is but a walking shadow"
swedish girl with loud
london tosser measures
his jokes against
her UK visa
he fills the language gap
with "doggy bag"
explains
"process of elimination"
as rewalking steps
to find the lost
five pound note
or doing the train again
for luckless keys
held tense clinked silence
maintains
maintains
"queen, you must ween knowledge
from the wings"

Poems for Lunch

     1

penetrative genius lock-picks concentration's hub
BIG ISSUE shoved between eyes & poems
when last week the same man announced it
with a tune : di-derrida
which made no difference & with more patience
but the same lack of money   still don't buy it
Thames prickled silver like silverfoil pricked
for recreational drug use seen once high
stop at the booksellers to flick a guide to fishing
by a quartet of the best anglers from the 1960's
first turned page has a balding picture in black & white
with text I won't forget:
"fish are not concerned with your comfort only their own"
which makes me think of a smoking jacket, slippers
& a hot fish pie
& the Thames bereft of dead fish, even, on their side
only amoeba explosions of soft silt mud
which brings footsteps & time into the realm of the synchronised
up the steps   to the poetry factory

2

capsules (millenium wheel) float in front of the sun
& suck the heat out of me.
I didn't know glass could do that.
rafters of a park bench place to think
head back to the wall
crumbles like oat into my hair.
hour of the cover version.
back to inherited roots.
if the houses were to burn again
it would probably be too hot
but we could always take our trousers off.
correlative to the man with a ferret on a leash
always   there is only/so much possible.
the next thing on the hot glass of sleep
where the wheel is a bangle of alchemist's phials
see the 8 on a digital watch
& hope there is no numbered structure
to the ways I'll wake & try to speak.
one revolution & the lunch break's gone.

Michelangelo Manufactured by the Murdoch Empire

Michelangelo as well, duplicitous
with a half-eye for what you wanted
BBC docu-dramatizes with freedom of evidence
jesus-figure plays him, *asides* to camera
he too knew what sells
faker—*poseur*—forger—
of a 1000 year old Cupid
plastered, coated in bio-yoghurt
& excrement
then buried underground
for six weeks, dug up
fizzing with authenticity

parable of the artist
the back of the beast that catches light
a side, facet, that eunuchs myth
strikes brilliance billiard ball white
Bacchus, androgynous
back-to-back to non-kosher Cupid
staggering asexually
(*Rupert Murdoch quip in a series of 2,000*:
"a genius on fleet street is someone
who is still sober at 12 o'clock")
over-erotic to sell
stomach swollen feminine
balls stumped penis like old spectators
at a cancelled game
re-seeing kitsch now dinner is on the table
shaping again, & still Riario—
the richest & most powerful in Rome—
rejects, shamed goggling
smashed over the curtained wall's plush baize
art unclassifiable in the cardinal's backlog

poem uploads to the Murdoch version
with a sudden sharp hot stink of FOX
genius of synchronicity
against the typos of time misspent
sitting at stool a'la Leopold Bloom
not reading, but tying shoes
& onto collectivist Wapping
[those offended by the hot name should look away now]
& *The Sun* like Stalinist lightbulbs to peasants
"devils' eyes"
suddenly milling for the country
I wonder why—says the non-believer—
what made them career a   yes
Post-Hillsborough
[look back now]

"SOMETHING IS ROTTEN IN THE STATE OF MURDOCH"
global pages veined marble
quarry building quarry
retro Cupid sells still
but Bacchus, bollockless
found backpaged & reproduced
in today's BETTERWARE catalogue

Père-Lachaise Cemetery

OSCAR WILDE

stone cock stolen
never yours anyway
transparent december
blue/light pilfered by black/light
kisses lipsticked to brick
hundreds like butterflies
scale pharaoh flying
every colour from mauve to pink
less permanent
than the white ford transit
parked in front

JIM MORRISON

biggest impotence
tooth-chipped gravestone
lizard king's baby piglet
unbutting up to mother's milk
every view a side-view
for the bigger grave in front
surely not you too
in the bunch of slaves
for the unasked for middle name
anchor: *douglas*

VICTOR NOIR

is that a skull in your pocket
or are you just pleased to see us?
more drainpipe than hosepipe
& the rose-vulva on your pocket
like a comedian's pocket
cast in slimestoned iron
where the flesh parts
its guilt throat of holy bread
in all those petticoats
riding your myth into cracked-light
fertility or eternity
whichever comes first.
listen mate: I'm sorry they shot you—
you've got a good sense of humour—
now you're only ever wet
on the outside of the trouser leg

MARCEL PROUST

graves are bigger than books, godfather
we sacrificed apollinaire & delacroix
to find you underscored black
half-an-hour through the pickled stone library
ring-a-ring-a-rebus
unpunctuated in the wind
even the teenage gravedigger didn't know where
you where or who you are
but there looking up
at the fin-de-siecle phonebox of mum & dad
echo no answer

Interpreting Flying Dreams

metaphor: was it a bird or a plane?

metaphor for whatever the metaphor was meant for.

& the meta-bit: apparently I was soaring above some mental blocks that had been weighing me down, I read it by coincidence in a magazine ten hours after the dream.

landed safe. ruby lake: deep-veined, oozing.
first fire made with the plush crack of an egg.
unformed still. no eye-jokes of fish.

it was uplifting.

A Piglet Imperialism

1

people with lollipops: watching:
fingers covered eyes horny lizards
it could cease to be—
reputation become a sandwich voucher

2

for Tony's palpitations

heart rigged to a monitor
slower it goes
fitter you are
lack of intelligence
will not ignite the body
into action
in response to tube
metal   adaptor
so beating faster
also measures
brain's parameters

3

wheel invented to transport the carcass
& only then metachanged into a symbol of fate
Boethius the bingocaller—

but enough

let us eat first & later, ruminate

Cititrix

://complaints : cascaded : into a form :
down into the hierarchy
signed & copied
duplicated in intray & folder
lost second imagined as silken drape
stapled to the back of the wrong form
& taken to the wrong room

(white noise code named 'river')

report brief defines possible
written questionnaires as a no-no
in the realms of dyslexic quantative research
& uses of computer languages
where there is always some "over-egging of the cake"
trainees taken to the control room
to watch us through reversible mirrors —

across a honeycomb of monitors   screen-by-screen
saw me turn to you   turn to you & laugh*

---

*   (later you would describe this as inner expression pressed into a pack of
    playing cards & passed through the hands of a hustler)

Two for the Zoo

HUON TREE KANGAROO

you've been abused   huggy one
emotional as the glass doll is deli-
cate   & huggy one your eyes
are chafed pink as pregnant underbellies
& you've turned to drink   huggy one
nose internal organ exposed
& call this number   huggy one
we're here to help you &
huggy one your huggy one hangs
out the pouch like a little huggy one
he'll be a monument to you   huggy one
we hope he grows up like you

ICHNEUMON WASP

that doesn't kill
but paralyses its prey to gorge on live flesh.
would a good & benevolent god allow for this?
you & me, we know this as work.

Flossing for Fishhooks

what's on?
an international forum
of religious leaders
discussing—
such news shouldn't come
between a man & his razor

:

"statistics show that 29% of atheists in the U.K. do pray sometimes"

:

camped at the back of a cross-city bus
pocket equipped
with a spoon & a pen

:

screen says:
"SORRY THIS SCREEN
IS OUT OF ORDER"

:

east london's biggest snowflake
drifts on the railtrack
o it is a feather
synthetic too

:

head sud dunked
in the virtual atlas
of the bathroom sink

Sky Tree Wank Star

coach rolls past a lake
flock formation   landscapes non-reproducible metal pixels
attempted to hammer to milk.

stars sifted network
of talcum   where we meet
settling into darkness around our bed.

tree rooted in expectation of tree
excites without adrenalin of the childclimber
imagined being seen at distances from branches.

immaculacies of neon
along golders green high street   causeway
of still-flickering registers and destinations.

under jacket   animal flummoxed
free-handed made decisions to touch
under clothes & stay hold of the beer
exacerbating the control you were in

        flock metal
      hammer network
       in branches
    registers destinations
    of flummoxed animals

intractable and twohanded

Post-Its

SOAP

came back into my life like something 'soft' you wouldn't usually think soft—say the sun through our window saying hello to the pillows

AUGUST

tied itself up in a brown-lined bag with just enough light for the cat to slip out

JOKES

that there's only so many formulas whipped by death-drive or Nietzsche's 'eternal recurrence' (before the hugging of the horse). & good plain-speaking northern ones like saying pre-sex "before we crack on love". I've been thinking of your theory that there will come a point in which the stock forms of jokes will each be given a number & to make one all we'll need to say is, for example, 'No. 48'. children will be taught the classics in school to prepare for society and non-set jokes will be taught in controversy. the kids will come to hate them more than poetry

SHOWERS

soapy wetness around was like carving the shape I'd desired & set white in the mind—each morning eyes opened to make sure it was still there & showered to confirm it

Network
after the first person to kill themselves live on the internet

he told you he was hardcore.
his space in the network
was at equal distances
to everyone else—that is
immediate—simplified
into the boolean dichotomy
of voyeurism. he was the
watched. as he eat the string
of pills he could have
explained so much about
the geo-technology of
network space being
harder   quicker   faster
along broadbanded
bandwidth, although in
the general sense an
analysis far short of
Dr Johnson Re.'network'
"anything reticulated or
decussated, at equal
distances with interstices
between the intersections"
short but Johnson did
not risk life to prove a
decision compensated for
in the technical common
sense of his final words:
"if I look dead give me a call"

running poet's heart thinks in free verse when it rains

ivy mask
streaks
down
wards

bullfrog

breathing

footslaps

on foxwatch

amber   orange
heat beneath
pavings
dimmed torchheads

trafficlights

containment

proverbs of colours

button pushed

WAIT

suggests difference made

we'll cross when
cars are passed

Case Study

brought you to the page & waited. the television leopard carried a dead heifer towards the v of the tree, & both fell earthwards before they got there.

what's the point of instinct bypassing thought if things go wrong? instead, there is writing: the inside of waiting: a tight-trousered spider in its own ministry trawls around a hamster wheel.

on the muted television, the leopard's mouth is pretty pink.

Garbagesleep

rapid eye movements
apparently
watching dreams' interior

licking outside walls a lover occupies

self parody of a parody of a ghost
in a shopping mirror—

you said sleep was sifting
crap, discarding—

what sticks precarious as a chapbook
read over a steaming bath

woke to the sound of a truck
approaching the street
from the big cake of sleep straight into debate—

do they want garbage bags or bags
to recycle?

The Other Tonight

COULDN'T SLEEP

insomniac for fleas in the eyebrows
sun's strobe hayflickering
stars & mites in the undereyes

cold western old as slo-mo
neck in three mirrors
talking barber

azure tuesday a much too big coat
slip-roads on broadband
here today here tomorrow

WORD-COUNT

wind through the wicker chair
knuckles rapped along a wall

inkbit drops, makes the *l* an *i*
disappears before the touch: flea.

is that your heart in the pressed keys
shed in the rain   drummed in

PUB TALK

one-way conversation installation
awesome awesome awesome
bluebird blackbird whitealbum
bla bla bla / bang bang bang
when the shit hits I'll be first to see it
to kop it in la la land up north
though closer scouse, a quick confession
before you go south:
on the day Hendrix died I had to ask who he was

THE OTHER TONIGHT

rearing children as barmen
from the age of three

apathy setting in the bones
like cooling chip fat

showing under the eyes
unpaid bills in shadowed halls

sitting hours for the double-portrait
unveiling an ear-lobe

adrenalin enhanced
by the three-way blink
the action / idea / the action—

whatever lifts your solipsistic skirt—

are we on a mission tonight
or just a mooch?

Babalaas

advertised
in the dictionary blurb
as being africaans
for 'hangover' which
if overheard downwind
at a busstop I might
have presumed to be
its opposite, say 'poured
running shit from the
mouth when pissed'
which I can buy &
use for thirty five
pounds with more
the same but different
/ better ones & not
mistake their unhydrated
anteriors as if I jumped
on the number 12
instead of 21 I wouldn't
be here telling you of
this having seen the
blurb on the wrong
bus wall triangled
in the forked rush
of the cross
roads

Dylan's Bust
reflections on Hugh Oloff de Wett's bust of Dylan Thomas in the Poetry Library

Bird shit in the bubble curls
when you lived outside
then forgotten   found
underground in the organisation's basement
plinthed & resurrected
head warble stalked on a tie
"kinda witty" said the american poet
who wasn't there when you didn't wake
in a pool of insides' soup
only meat-faced into conkers in a silk sick bag
that captures all rosette turd floor night-befores
& by day, hidden grit shifty between shell or shelled city
with burtonesque oratory played Mr Reliable for the BBC
Swansea you say? should disown you not cash in.

organics of mythology—at home
fingers chubby in a pickle dish
writing as if poems were organisms
palindromed as the worm
perfected edge to diamond edge:
job spun before the pissup's begun

in the groundwinking greycollared industry sized rain
hangover hooded
      your drink of choice "a half of bitter"
shameful basis for a hardrinking status to rests its bust on—
last night could be considered 'an average night' for me
seeing the top knocked off
4 bottles of export beer
3 large cans of guinness
1 bottle of wine
half a botttle of vodka

one poem for Caitlin   one post-rift apology poem
with you occupying the space between rift & apology
tiptoed down a self-warring alley
adding syllables to the cock, bitter-tugged
the narrator said was once stuck in a honey-pot—
words leaven flesh in conspiracy of bronze worthiness
being small as a man but aiming much higher
as so it goes great poets should
to fuck is to become & to come forever coming
in the splitting dank
                        open-endedly
tupping up to the moment above where
stars smashed brown jig the mosaic back
of a double-diamond label

The Garden Party

paparazzi flash over the gazebo
small fluster of motion or emotion sets off the nightlight
9st wideboy buckling under the weight of English
his pale mate could have been me if things hadn't gone
righter
all hold store for the pre-buffet downpour
psychic not so psychic to see
the smokedrawn panheaded cracked affair
& games of ships & submarines
down the jazz-ball braindrain
yapping ginger & white noise of the paw-mucked spaniel
having issues with the Gods of rain & thunder
Monty, Monty come here

Dance of the Victorian Remote Control

clop—clop—clop—clop

snuff

clop—clop—clop—clop

snuff

clop—clop—clop—clop

snuff

the victorians ran at night as well,
only slower

:

two on the corner can COMMUNE
in imagined glass nodes of the street
& still—for tonight at least—not be arrested

:

sex/city
dialectic
has replaced
desire/death
but when
the show's sound
disappeared
due to "technical
problems"
we heard wind

rattle pipes
like the last
kicked heels
in a *danse macabre*

:

morning you are winking into a boiling kettle I wanted to warn
you it might burn but wanted to see if you found what you were
looking for

:

bull's nose
of the double doors
signposted
twice
with "FIRE DOORS"
& "PRIVATE"
walked
waytowards
wanting
what
wasn't
onanism of fire
liking itself
more
than others

:

"housing-estate suave"

:

snouted authority
rubber corridors
pornography hazed
reproductive art

elevator, broken

we walk

into a pilgrim's
palm of advice
against the grain
as diced chicken

"what it is is
life is life
so this is this, it's
not that"

once again,
thanks john

:

a mid-century letter from the seaside

go go gadget mindfuck

is it someone, when the door opens
worse in afternoon light
dishwatering cubed glass—

hinge, breeze, slope?

I will shop for us today
simple provisions
then do wheelies up the highstreet
with no hands for bags—

& tonight, eat falling sand from a hairbrush

Progress Poems

so sing your praise of progress and of the Doom Machine
Bob Dylan

Everything that perfects itself by progress also perishes by progress
Blaise Pascal, Pensees

To them, globalization (which typically is associated with accepting triumphant capitalism, American style) *is* progress
Joseph Stiglitz, 'Globalization and its Discontents'

Humanity tied the shoes of progress, that enormous child
Arthur Rimbaud (Transl. By Wyatt Mason)

DNW: Have we made progress?
Manuel Castells: You and me have made progress, many of our friends have made progress. We're more intelligent and creative, not wealthier, but doing quite well. But I think the most important thing is the loss of meaning. We don't know where we are, we don't know what is the world around us, we don't know how to relate what is happening to us to what we want.
Manuel Castells interviewed September 1998

Nothing avails: one *must* go forward—step by step further into decadence (that is *my* definition of modern "progress")
Friedrich Nietzsche

it's stupid when all the astrologers burglarize the stars
Blaise Cendrars (Transl. By Ron Padgett)

Oh, but a man wants to get on in the world!
Does he then? does he really?
Progress, you know, we believe in progress!
Do we really? Well I never! fancy now, fancy that!
Progress!
D.H. Lawrence

The best thing about the Human Spirit is that it never gives up, and that is how we make progress.
Tony Blair

#1,502: *letter to rupert murdoch regarding his smile*

wrote: *mouth   lips   jowls*
only *gob* would do
pith pitted
ruined orange
serene smile
floated surreal
like a penis on a woman—
slick flick
of a sick fish
hungryfull
pike smirk.
agreed?

say you'll print me.

601: *punk*

putting the kitsch into kitchen
johnny rotten extolling churchill's heroism
cut & paste first word being *dada*
leaves like stick insects drop-click on the two-inch tabletop
dry as a beach found eardrum
touch the black rose it puffs to dust

better to die with your feet swinging to *rawhide*

1,991: *kiss my arse or I'll kick your head in*

public sideburns

starched brown suits

interview raining
technology's constellations
furred lights car-sized   blind
& roll to the ducts like ballbearings
eyes everywhere but the questioner
headlamps down each sidestreet

public sphere non-absorbent
baubles frail as eggshells
or perspex veneers frosted
as bathroom windows
curly Qs of questions made dialectical
                      in statistical polls
pins of adrenalin
asked straight out & then
were you listening anyway?

threat to bomb
all the way to the bottom a russian-doll
equations of right transformed by daybreak
relativity removed
so, like, it can't be a moving target
                if it's got a name
(Bush): "when a mushroom knows it's a mushroom
it doesn't taste the same".

in on democracy's moneyshot
managers with managers
their managers higher managers

them leaders of government
meshed precise as fishscales
the way things are
& so say all of U.S.

11: *wittgenstein*

> *"you really get such a queer connexion when a philosopher tries to bring out the relation between name and thing by staring at an object in front of him and repeating a name or even the word 'this' innumerable times".*
> 'PHILOSOPHICAL INVESTIGATIONS'

tried on the first thing in sight—

bottle. bottle bottle bottle bottle bottle bottle bottle bottle bottle bottle bottle

this this this this this this this this this this

CLICK: bottle top turreted tower sprung up on the vertical edge of the village of language

vittel

1,336: *1938*

it is 1938.

the england football team have just saluted the nazi leadership before a match in berlin.

it was suggested by the chief of the F.A. & —being working class —the impassioned elbows automaticed as window wipes.

mickey mouse has subtly softened from the sharp-toothed, brawny, *violent* creature he was before, to a provider: offering escapism through magic & nature looped to the lymph-nodes of classical music.

from now on—until the advent of punk—there will be far less for the working class to associate with.

227: *lunch-break powernap:*

world's first & biggest ringing phone condensed
into a mobile—you woke me bastard—
what is this fidgeting slurping
fish goofed in the shallows
tooth/ceramic chink over a soup bowl?

902: *graduating*

batman suited chessboard

pissing knowledge font

finger to the crowd

& into the Job Hunt:

reflection dreaded in glassy billboards

1,927: *annual conference:*

corporate red
repigmented
very corporate
green / dream
elevator job—
which floor
please—
brain's finger
swims becomes
staircase
outside bison's
dance protest
in shredded
shrieks of
pink licks-up
the joined
luminescent 'I's
of policemen
helmet-dotted
useless as a
fart by e-mail
hitting a firewall
or tits on a bull

inside the
stone beast
conferencing
goes on
despite the
stink bomb
crawled under
our door
from the
briefcase-activist
reverse plongeur

day sun dies
red & ruddy
like a bloody
runny egg
between slices
of glass
box marked
'greek delight'
is litter-dropped
bin top
in case of
future re-use

1,394: *the allies*

knows no silvers or golds
us: allies copper-fastened friends

743: *thatcher & the brighton bomb*

north-south division
(terrorism) chimney
brickwork (democracy)

plug/clock
video digital
music box
inside an egg
decorated

2:53

roof lifts
hotel unzips
steel-teases
target ceiling
like a pendulum

(dennis quick
quick dennis—

yellow fondue
of policemen
interview
C=O=N=F=E=R=E=N=C=E
goes on
response braced
is that all you want
will that be all john?

tebbit dreams
whiteblue virgins
of feeling

MPs create
cabinet
5-bar gate
& counting
cabinet's hearts
unlock & ad
renalin flock
for the Big Job

tebbit sleeps
in blue pyjamas
red shed on
the bedspread
peppered in
cement fire
men blow
from the
chalked head—

she speaks

she speaks

two public
hail marys
instant sleep
throat strokes
in soft
black gloves
doesn't mill
about to
miss its
Ace-black
chance

1,492: tHE sTAND-dOWN cOMEDIAN:

white navel of the sun burns through orange curtains

ceramic seahorse seen through steam

suds   settles   sleep

breathes the dream-breath: show begins—

remembering the pain—

185: *search engines*

snowed-in white screen
with 'no hits'
asks
did you mean?
which you try
(though you didn't)
& still returns
'no hits'

838: *the class divide*

> yeh, it's te do wid copyright regulations—ignore da, i'm always blackframed round ere—i can read ye de poem dough or give ye some background on it if you'd like. i've come across dis before in a new-historical context so it won't be a problem for me to elp ye out if ye want me to? i'm quite interested in de kind of seamless dialectics if it anyway, de way de worldview & de speech are de blower & de glass bowl in one go, if ye know wha i'm sayin like. dere's more to it dan meets de pig-ready eye. or anoder way: de book grouts between its bricks wid a tongue-hungry trowel. cleans out its grate wid its own airs & graces. yeh, yeh, course ye can speak—just let me close meself in—

sweetheart, I can't grasp *a word* of what you are saying

764: *painting the sky:*

sore blue ink run under skin
eyes ungripped as flip-flops
slip off moss sea-green tinge
cumulus polystyrene padded
umbilical streaked black over
the next town watercolour
forked with a fossil fin, big
shadowed gulls half-baked
still cold & pink in the middle

#1,291: *beyond iraq*

defending space
the ongoing project
colonization with
out religion
what is that
white thing
in the home-cam
grey drizzle
like something
        nasal
colon spinning
into a ball
& down into
a field by
some horses

800: *ivor cutler*

see you next time he said I said not
if I'm like this [turned my back] he
said then I'll be like this [turned his
back] & there might be mirrors in front of us

he said there might be mirrors in front of us
I said not if I'm like this [turned my
back] he said then I'll be like this
[turned his back] see you next time I said

1,772: *a drunk man compares teenage pregnancies to a horse chestnut*

foodwood:
dimple-scarred
tooth-bitten
two-tone mahogany
smooth as mothballs
                      in the thread
or cobwebs, damp—
socketed in the palm
live-fused
in the pocket's clothed spider
watching

pale giant on the scaffold of the pram
ill-initiated
age crossed-dressed
                      projection
one life/two ages
seen at once
the child & not so child
now hole for the begging string
they want you to be:
asker, statistic, road-watcher.
known matter
read in rings
spooning sympathies
to a toothless winge.

youth to youth
like the new tooth
too soon, precocious
forked before the old
unready to soften its root
& stuck that way for all days:

talisman of dissatisfaction
mnemonic for 6 o'clocks
litmus tested in caffeine, smoke.

& that cry of amazing ventriloquism.

192: *suburbs train*

double-dinged bell & the post-london
suburbs train departs—same place
names plummet slacken & resurface:
WATERLOO again on the NORTHERN
LINE saying it slow through the thick green frieze
city in the mind crumbles like a caryatid
reglossed in emulsion, fields golden black
stubbled with mishaped cows
children watch to learn the language
of their own quickness of travel:
to laugh & try to moo through dummies

659: *cleaning habits:*

& for some—to wash & clean up—is to
piss their own shit-stains from the toilet pan

#255: *darwin*

1

greatest mystery
story ever
inquisitorial simulacrum
copies of copies
without a template
even & squatting
twelve inches in front
a train speeds
through the station
splashes rain
onto an open book

in a group

starched brown suits

waves skein beach
into tongues
epiphanies of gulls
grandchildren
sliding down
history's banister
on an invented seat
self-made
with a little brake
could see sea & through
bigger kings than
all your kings
arcane prints
of copyright signs
along the sand
named beach

2

missing piece
phone ringing
continuously
in an empty house
or hotel
observing treats
in the dark
holding the line's
montage of callers
iguana & pig
evolution's table
down on all fours
dissolves darkness
into furniture
maids move
in other rooms
stop cogs of the clock

666: *surprise visitations*

last phone dring snagged-up sleep
waiting like a running dream
on the thames   ansamachine says so
is it waterloo & the glitterglass sound
of the 'box of toys' pissing on my chips
or tomorrow's hushed northern echo of departure
like wind through steel which is which the city is
at Euston

592: *theatre of war*

tophatted fintailed fish
slime-slaps across the stage
in *the theatre of war*
ENCORE!
ENCORE!
explained into the microphone
as the guilty first wife of the ape
mouth above
nose above
eyes
& efficient duplex
of the gullet & windpipe
save the chance to choke
in us by virtue
of the selfsame lobed fish
that side-stepped ashore
& so the cycle comes full-circle folks
as Bush says to Blair
come on in, the water's lovely

1,906: *bonnie & clyde*

on the run from the cops this life
of crime   turns me on
snakes wrapped around ankles
red indians know our evil   instinctively
each town appears in green neon
& people complain of bad head
but it makes me glad   yours

#374: revisionist theories

age of revisionist agendas

consonants rev a furred engine over the tongue

upside-down photograph of the author

looped & flaked under truth's scratch & sniff

433: *the jogger*

twelve minutes & forty-eight seconds — not bad —
two miles backpacked —
biro heart press on paper pavement's wet:
harder it's pushed slower it goes.
low impact the one businessman described the day
to the other, though april had sprigged through his hair
    foolishly.
dad — sorry — *father* has cramped his speech & I'm up to this:
words candy-stringed for playground artillery
blank flag wrinkled as puppyfat
smooths to a flutter & colours
regulated to the heart's pentameter

   iamb   iamb   iamb

171: *mobile phone games in first class*

suits: closed oysters
washing powder stained
wrists' nests
famished fingers
baldwhite chick heads
thumbs the fighters
puffpastried into reflex—
bling bling—
green screen
brick-a-brack snake
right angles
into apples

1,333: *defining genre:*

kitsch: abject criticism or description?
they asked what music you said 'riot girl'
you were dissatisfied they were dissatisfied
I thought of the roaring girl & a lifted skirt
the what-came-next safe cage of history
bung   spiders' legs   shaving line
stepped to the left of the escalator to walk up
downwards metal-webbed in repair
sounded like travel   vroom   vroom

555: *george w. bush*

hacking memes   okay
gave up the ruddyred liquor
couldn't control the leaside road
gave up too slavering 60's pipedreams
follow: boots to shins shirts three quarter
the texan way   what's under as important
as what's on top
follow me up from toe to tonguetip
camerastop to describe
each pitstop to armpits
easier than leaders' names
lioncourage of my face can't be aped
the rest is all in the mind.
him   crawfished stiff
stiffing the world
I won't make do with symbolic
brains homes hearts
balloondrifting & shoeclicking
believe me folks   when I get to oz
I'm going to look inside that smoked machine
till I find the real thing

302: *indexing blighty*

plural
       possible   from   stems
possible   plural
       from   stems
from   possible   plural
    stems
stems   from   possible   plural

87: bakhtin's smoking habits

"There is also M. M. Bakhtin, the Russian critic and literary philosopher. During the German invasion of Russia in World War 2, he smoked the only copy of one of his manuscripts, a book-length study of German fiction that had taken him years to write. One by one, he took the pages of his manuscript and used the paper to roll his cigarettes, each day smoking a little more of the book until it was gone."

PAUL AUSTER, 'THE NEW YORK TRILOGY'

unwrote rolled smoked
each page vanity daubed
as air guitar
put in
"RUSSIAN FORMALIST"
and "GERMAN OCCUPATION"
168 hits in 0.07 seconds
like a trooper my wife said
holed in the brown room
visitors virtuous in gas masks
one leg gone not a problem after all
nowhere to run   to
work/world dialogue self-enclosed
name jokes done
I eat those words
what's more important
when you're going to die
a good book or a good smoke?
turgenev's   tolstoy's
then mine   rolled like rizlas
german fiction 1880–1939
backwards to the titlepage
        bildungsroman

[73]

21: *the martyrs*

believing the word until the tongue turns to bread
muteness (mutates) conviction
breaking the back of flesh
& offering
        lies
                that rise like yeast in broken tongues

1,803: *the lads*

super kings, discolighted
blackbilious cudboys
of inhouse take-aways
under ceiling rashed
random shifted
rainbow rays.
doof doof—lager
glass dinked joke—
mushroom swollen
in through the thumbs
up door: boy on crutches
to the round of applause bar.
check shirt kisses
pink shirt too close to the lips
all slows, pre-fight:

complete 3-sixty of the mobile in the palm

shot downed in the thumb-thimble

message in lipstick smeared across glass

awake in the is it still yesterday

457: *a perfect imagist poem*

dry summerleaf drops on southbank
stone—stood on sounds like plastic:

someone checks their back pocket for visa

409: *on the night bus:*

3-chord jingle
sells more than the album
johnny foreigner
shoves past the referee
never on the night bus
without someone
throwing up
halitosis hails
the attention
shit it's left it's
light on now
someone's in the back
before I've noticed
ratface forked into a
silver pickedevant
disgorging words
from a far-off throat
about experimentation
at the expense of
communication
being an absolute
indulgence of the
bourgeoisie

702: *the union*

brides or bodies?

I'm calling the union

freestylin

you can change the subject
I won't lose sense of smell

cow

#959: *television networks*

answer me of the pigeons in trafalgar sqaure. tourists flock to see them on a yearly ratio that outnumbers the birds. each time one humps its grey jumbo into a gutter a camera goes flash. *but they're only pigeons.* voyeuristic feeding leads to shitting in endless cycles & its poisoned emulsion is eating the benches, consuming the architecture. the real tourist attractions. rats with wings/harbingers of disease. they have rights to live & should live. *but they're only pigeons.*

the dumpties of the five embryos. candles ready lit, only one the real child. the unwilling father neither consenting or lost but unforgiving in the owning. to her they are the green bottles of her only chances hanging precariously on fertility's broken wall. she will teach mother earth to suck eggs if it kills her. the pop soap jury are out demanding a speech: *adopt! adopt!*

the pill in the aqua that kills the nerve-worm forever. one man solipsistic slalom throught the straights of switzerland. to arrive at the place, the very white place. walls cushioned, clean, not quite bright enough to ignite the will to live. a monet, so blue. & her, the harlequin who holds the glass at the bedside (part-time, 26 hours, full benefits incl. 17 annual paid days plus bank holidays) cannot proffer. that would be murder. her kind burdened face the last you'll see. tea breaks float through a cumulus explosion of semi-skimmed & then back to the day's flat bronze. rose cheeks perennials. glass bleached.

time recorded: 4:17

#1,857: *media coverage*

tuneful toot of the white funbus past the sign marked
iraqi border

blue arrows: media map: day 11: halfway to baghdad

rivulets of paint over a wrestling ring floor

england grandslam win & a brown stout downed in one

1,687: *backseat activism*

while mother was drinking her tea—sloop!
emptied her bags & explained
the third world corruption of brands
which she promised never to buy again.

down the boozer with the lads:
I said that we're all basically the same
though living in different shaped houses.

tried to call from a phone booth
without a phone.

next morning to sweat out the toxins
turned the t-shirt's logo to the chest
& shadowboxed

328: *management styles:*

aficionado (he was) of MBWA
(Management By Walking About)
which he did
as his coiled hip
dipped in (for weight) on his withered stick

1,531: *internet death of chris mccabe*

death of my metaname
on the internet
shot change/opened page
I'm feeling lucky
first hit in blue then red
same name with dates
commiserations
though supporter of the *other* team
me red him blue
own goal sunk
in the opened link
mutable/under the surface
cursor levitating cross
in "the invisible web"
undisputed (now) fact
ghosted in ironed underpants

#278: *genetically modified*

> "Earlier this week, the conference heard that aborted foetuses could be harvested for eggs & infertile women could one day give birth using a womb transplanted from their mother"
>
> METRO JULY 2003

mother was a dead foetus

microlens egg
slipped out the me-eye

looked for her:

sneaky corridors

bourgeois haircuts

& looked face on at terrible desire:
greasy starlings
attacked a chicken drumstick

tiger-backed butterfly
I liked (more) behind glass

       this
       slip
        of
       ser
       end
       ipid
       ity

sister   reverse   russian doll
gave me all   her matter
already I was seven months older
& ageing

        wordless
as a milkless pap

expunged into the world
like the shadow of the moon
into a mouse's earhole

819: *barflies*

eyes' barbell glint
gunmetal
or dreadnought grey
in these parts
we call a cunt
someone we like
whether drink
mixing fox
with a finger
in each pie
or heavystubbled
snow-hedged
stout hedgehog
tipple-familiar

for signs: read
icecube mirrors
made stars

look: for the wink
that takes root
in the plumed smoke's
growbag

526: *some propaganda*

this is propaganda
if you agree
read on
if you disagree
read on
his name
spelt backwards
is what he is
nomenclature caricature
in palindrome
enclosed is a mirror
hold it against
the mind's eyes' radio
for
FALL
OF
SADDAM
read
LLAF
FO
MADDAS
water
will
follow

972: *pre-reading reception:*

on the list—in the blackringed reception area—
step over as a waitress asks permission into focus
carrying a silver tray of beige pastries.
shout: shit: I've missed the custard creams.
arena eyeballs the finger-lickin pink of me.
sweetheart listen, they are cous*cous* croissants.

#189: *vincent van gogh*

17 red buses counted on the bridge (waterloo)
3 & a bit bar gates in the margin next
the sketch of quick black bare branches
& scratch-circles of tree leaves—
setting the scene with speed, impersonal—
9 nation's flags breeze-warbled in colour
in(decipherable) out the globe
with four colours of the eyes
like birthday handkerchiefs
folded to suit the suit, say on such a day
azure   auburn   ochre   pink
only remains to afford the suit
here comes the whole-sum-lump
to spud punch the air—ME:
self-named identity depression
for my next trick will say it
buses sink/grid-locked old party things
run through the view like a blood-cough

1,111: *ezra pound*

"In 1945 he was arrested by the US Army and held in an army
prison camp at Pisa, where he was placed in solitary confinement in a large
outdoor cage. He was later allowed the privacy of a small tent within this
cage"
THOM GUNN

"And the blue-gray glass of the wave tents them,
Glare azure of water, cold-welter, close cover."
'CANTO II'

Shock-stripped light
Branched the ribcage-cage
Enters the cave
Cripple-must basement
                   Heat-swirl
Here the favourite hole, forward
To white ring views
Rose-brick rain-petals
& them with their smirk-eyes:
I want to see
If they want to make faces.

911: *self-referential poetics*

he said these poems
whistle down the u-bend
over the shoulder
back to the arsehole

1,174: *industrial reminder*

mangled waffle of stonebridge & pylon

(N.B. consult running 'quarry' of images here—)

literal reminder
of undone danger:
half-smoked cigarettes
on railway tracks
                       & a sign:
                               NO
                               BALL
                               GAMES

850: red label classification in the letter library

A: behind the tepee, pen scythe-swooped & a blood red sun.

B: dreaming bubblegum. strawberry.

C: cat's smile in a campfire.

got promotion before I got to **D**.

1,061: *sunday morning*

they said any civilian damage would be put
right it would be a triumph for collective
human spirit & medical science so they
brought the boy the prosthetic limb & he
asked would it grow they said no & then
the director of the limbless society showed
him *his* plastic leg the boy asked could he run
he said it's the only thing I can't do then the
boy turned to the doctor & said thank you
you have given me great hope for the future

#133: *the office*

peter principle of the palate
uncrisp tick in the middle
the dampened pendulum

50: james joyce

"abced-mindedly"
forgot you
day finger-poked
in dots
of question marks
doubled-up
as fullstops
minger-choked air
from planet uran
ating woman
for lick her
went to fatty'o
fingerme's
& put the coloured
balls in the
triangle as states
the rules
cliches smattered
across the baize—
red & green unseen—
I was so excited
sat in the sunshaded
shitehouse for
three days
pissing out my arse

471: *a particularised history of cocaine*

rattled the schoolboy box joint of his/tory
cells of the phone multiplied in his ear
slipped through the gap & nobody heard
his shout, first word thought was the longest
he knew—

king stein, kidneys shrinking to shallots
sleep talking—o you—side-splitting tumour
& progressing to the beak spoon slim as a bird's bone
feeding, soup-starved to the nostril's mouth
back to novel-cum-manual, slapping
the face of each page, quick, for her
one eye on the window's black mirror
for the panning machete of car light
making an epiphany of white
heralding lady heroine's arrival
in origami bookmark collars
threatening blue flames at the first point of exhalation,
    movement

1,002: rome; a play in eleven lines

(takes place at the general enquiry desk of the bus-stop)

heron: you wouldn't get away with it then
    when community was a slug's crop-circle
    & the silver-foamed saliva of a copper in your ear

leather: they can do what they want on the streets of india
    cultures of dud cities & relationships
    pens with no insides

heron: today has been beautiful but tomorrow will be
    beautifuller
    scooped-out pink on a perfect blue
    rome will flick on in their minds like the moving brick of
    a lizard

299: *thank you tony*

for our lessons
in time & space
your talks
were immediate
but his were
pre-recorded
the face to
film set
to name race
slightly different
each time
but like fancy
dress all
the same &
all those planes
so lovely down
the runways

1,463: *michael jackson*

palimpsest of myself
octopus-minded
many gripped
& disneyfaced
in the snowfield
me & blanket
turinshrouded
pianofingered
all white-keyed
life we lead
me & blanket
kindersurprised
white-on-the-inside
& there—
plasticsouled
pillcradled surprise
like a child
nasal-clustered
low profiled
in public's eyes
priest's confessional
sisters of islam
& *plath* I don't know
he makes me speak
little man on the make
to finish this for you
blanket:
moon disc
with my past faces on

#986: *winter*

blow flesh warm to warm the bone cold.

up the steps to the work desk.

to say "today it is cold" is to rise above the body.

to joke about this is to leave the body behind.

1,600: *in england*

we call a spade
a fucking spade

hide our monkey parts in the bath
in case anyone walks in

dilate pores over the green sheen
of sprout steam

take antecedent to spring
dr samuel carter's miracle anti-ageing elixir of youth

watch the balding boys get on the bus

tracking crackles into focus

branding barber
studying footage of the one-legged invincible black knight

soaking still scraping the gravy dish
black as oil from railway sleepers

running brook   same   as running brook 926 AD

careers selling cigs to kids
or chief squealer at the pig-initiation class

701: *maslow*

sandstudded tongue
creaked upper of a nazi boot
(bird with a broken wing butting the glass ceiling)
antennae-knocker sucking for the flush unfound door
hidden somewhere along the brick-chained base of the social pyramid

1,094: *billy the kid retires, marries & turns to poetry*

back in the wildwooded north-west
outlawed at the inlaws
cock soft-triggered
secure latched.

when ripped desire's jeans: gold-rushed loins.

thinking revenge, revenge
dreaming your hand
smoothed along my
sunned forearm &
most dangerously
close to the
writing hand

1,744: *the hippocritopotamus*

"WELL DONE"
stitched seed
keep me in mind

accept all
handshakes
as gold hunt

initiated smiles
metatags dropped
transparent politics

The Reality

842: wittgenstein 2

"'Stand roughly there'? Suppose that I was standing with someone in a city square and said that. As I say it I do not draw any kind of boundary, but perhaps point with my hand—as if I were indicating a particular spot"

'PHILOSOPHICAL INVESTIGATIONS'

not there but *here*.

that someone is you.

peace shatters in birdflight overhead: more whirr than flutter.

this exercise obviously exists of no fixed meaning.

november   crisp. cross over a square of city through a named threshold (e.g. 'the bricklayers' arms') into smoke   ethereal   as setting fog. ludicrous   allowing alcohol into this.

soon we will have the courage to attempt definitions.

#1,231: *shopping*

leaves on the trees confused
the zigzags of the bridge
black daredevilry quick on
motorcycles lose the image
as legs slack to the side
like defunct fish fins
approaching traffic lights
see misted through visors
underhull sea-lights
& the shop I'm asking for
blazed in the same colours
as every other shop around here
(every other shop around here)
I would have answered when
they asked for money but
they'd already looked away
anyway safe in what tourists
don't know, that those at the
back of bus stops board first

170: *the divorce rate*

lanky shire horse
of the wife
poodlehaired
lobster-pink face
shot frozen
side-eyed
sly statistics
approach.
rough patch
of the honeymoon
delicate-edged
six & a half inch
crystal high-heels
& won't pay
to reverse the charges
on a past vasectomy
to travel back
to the place
of having children
to have his manhood
ripped open
you can't claim for that
you know
& talking is different
from fantasizing.
wedding day's
mantlepiece-arched mind
still standing around

in starched brown suits

then this:
pink torpedo
of last night's
lipstick &

rolled silver
eyelids of
popped paracetamols.
old marriage kids
don't like new dad's
pissy-iced persona
ringing up mum—
how can people fall out of love—
& hanging up

1,192: *osama bin laden*

until we accept
bin laden escaped
into the animated
set of scooby doo
we'll live in the
midlands of history
& when the pesky
kid lifted mask
comes to show
say, saddam hussein
we can't seem to be
shocked or we'll
give the plot
away

The Smog: *London Poems*

The London Weather News

7:18
digits seagreen
in the water
of another country

bare feet
tacked
to lino

outside "gales of between
50 and 70 miles an hour
that could uproot trees"

water cistern vies with wind
think "chumbles"
along pipes

in the bedroom
your dreambreathing
like kids' splashes
in the shallows

bed ripples warm
all the way to the window
a shadow winds depth—

7:30
wake & dress
in reverse dream logic

walk out of the door—

the shadow has moved to the city

which you walk towards, into a facing wind

Untitled

inbetweeness of being

jam jar blue

neither fish nor fowl
but tree-frog

across the waves we'll call 'crisp'
shallows amphibious confusion
lens hones in
on clams opening   bruised lips
black as audio tape & a sound, brusque—

"CUNTS"

Blaine in a box
ballot-box of Blair

across communties we've travelled to this city

into a matrix of transparencies

Three London Poems

TREES AT HACKNEY WICK

black ventricled bare branches
child-angry scrawl on wax paper
plastercracked neutral chalk-white sun
softedged silhouettes through railings
up concrete steps to the overhead bridge
(*good morning london*) & look back—
trees have gone mad, branched up   up
trying to stop sky falling on them
blind-fanning locusts from their hair.
                    (enters the drunk's
swinging giblet of spit stuck to the lip
handle of horror rolls in the cinemascope bus
                    & everyone looks

PALIMPSEST

station's manual digital clock clacks
directs the scene: take   take   take
8:03:46   47   48   49   50

below district line's deliriously driven drinks' trolley
low black london orange-flecked
like hot scattered ash
reflection undissolves transparent
extinction's memories of the shallows—
silhouette woman unknown & alone:
I have been looking straight through you

JUBILEE LINE

pubic triangle of the nest in the branch bones
barbed wired white disc
tumbles unripe fruit from a ripped net
& window-lolls like a tongue of boiled ham.
thought   shocked-sleep
aerials parallaxed by lamp-light
three minutes & forty-eight seconds
polyester dreams
woke where east is the turned-out glove of west
       & everywhere burnt silver

Zone

at the helm of the lightmachine bus
enter first through the on-come glass
into operating system white
heads down in handheld gadgetry
with a springing sound herein described as DIGI-BOING
we step off the bus into map zoned 2
having dogeared the tube route with the double-decker
which means now we have more money
but are in more danger
lost in the blueshrieked glass peacock's back
of South London

Jogging in the Country Park

stop to piss
three weeks
of stella
& cheap vodka

mud laughs
wet froth
flower-like

grey squirrel
under railings
enquires
feels this is part
of her daily order

when this stops
I will no longer
belong

∽

white plastic
on red brick
stipulates
lest we forget
smallish one—

LONDON BOROUGH
OF BARKING
AND DAGENHAM

Any Normal Day in Dagenham

metal tooth chatter of garden gates

wind rips up through the road: car disappears in the ear

still floral-netted day swelled surreal to two plumed
black cortege horses big as terraces: wet glass eyes on me

pounds of shire shite disappeared the *s* on the disabled bay

brown beer-bottle glass out-rolling the stones

although my mouth was hooped into an *o*
it was the wind blowing in that made it whistle

East London pulled the pall on the weather
meaning bring in your dead but only our clothes were wet

wearing shades as day greys to punctuate falling pebbledash

pulling to repair washing-line pulley
                                    once monthly wash of blues
                                            & greens
pirated fly transmogrified human

                over the wet deck of the raft of the medusa

London Migration Sequence

suds of tail lights at traffic lights

submerged flakes of last night's lipstick
runs down a wineglass into murky dishwater.

all top lights on red.

seeing incensed pupils dilated

aftershave indistinguishable from perfume

first autumn leaf   crushed moccasin
powders into putty cracks.

the city tonight: the way you love sharks
but wouldn't like to be alone   its jailhouse of teeth.

once near complete bauble of the smashed wineglass

:

new whiteminded associations of you:
firm bed & undersheets polyester tight
with the novelty of a holiday camp
which is what is dreamt: family close
over the bridge where rabbits froze.
do you remember when I stayed out all night
& you pulled down our room
how good it felt to put it right?

then woke to mistake the liverbird for a griffin.

its filthy money hordes.

:

this city is exciting at first & then becomes more
than most can take
it is not having control over streams of images
magazines reproduced on linen
& trawled under the surface of a lake of sea-water

:

do

do no

do not o

do not obstru

do not obstruct the do

do not obstruct the doors

:

unfashionable building of the house season
september in a reversible jacket
soft dugs
of blue summer drying into folded receipts
as the bet goes down in the sunless zone

:

northern retreat cuts through years:
fizzing near silent sunday nettles
crosswrapped over concrete columns
broke open with ochre   rust   copper
wires we jumped over
in the slate flat budweiser grass
searching for the non-boredom summer us

:

bigger now   through freehouse glass
when you disappear minutes together
I look into the unloanable books
drawn each time to *a guide to the nervous system*
by someone, think "john gibson"

:

world service undercackles modestly on the portable TV in the room's left corner up from the double-bed. wine is so cheap here. take the silver elevator down into the dishbowl of paris. boulevard sant michel; quartier latin. into december relieved from the sultry hotel. first night here: journey's only description a microscopic one from the fin end of the intestinal tract of a rainbow trout seeing clear—upriver. I buy yours from mcdonald's but I won't, not even in paris. cross over into the cheaper meat equivalent. tagged in the anywhere I'm rushing to share it with you. back to the hotel the guard responds to the buzz & lets me in. I hold up the mcdonald's bag like a pass or excuse & up to our room the cardkey won't open the door & you let me back in—

you were asleep where have I been

:

through floral glass

day swells & colours

like an amoeba

digitised

on a plasma screen

:

"DOWN WITH LENIN AND HORSE-MEAT
GIVE US THE TSAR AND PORK"

:

tony pokes the pony up a horse track

we eat the same our parents eat

:

rife selfishness / navel concern
numb fuzzing comfort like a dentist's waiting room
when one of you is coming out from the chair
& the other, younger sibling is going in

then to wonder how you turned out as you did

:

bond deep   as looking down into a clear night sky
reflected in black oil
above & below   suspended freely

:

allegorical approach

ghosts wear the ghost cloak
to spook but look
like the ghost impersonators

:

inscription on the ascribed pot
shop in the place it always was (different name)
on the day off they gave
at the odds they offer
to write it out like a prescription signature
reflected through perspex as autograph

:

walking upstairs
I'm thinking
you're carrying
unopened mail
but when the sound
of a nose blown
arrives I know
your hands are free

:

deepan americana in Essex

rows of baseball caps at the pie & mash shop

new neon route   wet night

running & cussing at shadows

mongoose of a leaf's shadow

evidence of time passed in unrewound tapes (overdue)

at the crossroads marked

pizza hut / blockbuster

lit football shirt red & coldshoulder blue

that's not right

but the night you see the night

is alert to this

The Hutton Inquiry

Andrew Mackinlay: "Have you ever felt like a fall guy? You have been set up, have you not ?"
David Kelly: "I accept the process".
(David Kelly interviewed by Andrew Mackinlay of the Foreign Affairs Select Committee)

"many dark actors playing games"
(David Kelly, from an Email written hours before his death)

22 May—a meeting
in the Charing Cross
Hotel

precise 6:07
broadcast
a week later
(*Today*)

past summer
waiting / happening
the way
"faster"
shouted from a moving
car
sounds slow-motion

processes of summer
revealed veil-by-veil—is someone getting married? no, but——

glass cabinet transparent against the sky
tenfolds of adipose flesh disappearing slow as ageing
a man rises hedgehog-headed, puffin-eyed—
spectacle of what the fuck, how the fuck of fuck all
tension perspective—television or tower bridge—
cheery suspense, like a fat stolen bus

Charing Cross Hotel—one appletise, one coke—
4 pound 15 price of asphyxiation
Gilligan claims back expenses
without receipt for suggestion sliding into headline
time: a fact (one week before release)
name: a fact (Campbell)
touch-typed into electronic personal organiser
in the network buslane delayed down the Strand
towards Whitehall, opening TB's emails marked 'confidential'
witnesses, accounts, decisions not made but generated step-by-
    step
hayflickering like degenerative flesh
cells unreproducible
linked to public forum website, accessible at last

at the angular centre:
marathon man sucks the pipes into the bag

composed

unelected

weaving

best game
ever
cursor like
a creature
works
its way
through a
life's-work
document
breathes up
through gaps in
text—
it is not
how long
it takes
to make it
to the top
that measures
the success
or the document's
worth

one man's notion
of "right" turned
into chip-wrapper
facts—it is a dark
unfair thing for
people to have
on their hands

Dr Kelly described
as "chaff"
which to a defence expert
is what destroyers
send out
to deflect incoming missiles

Tony says the *mail on sunday*
story added
"booster rockets"
to the allegations—

let us go back one more time
boys
since I last played these games
has been so many
unmetaphorical years

similarity in appearance
between Dr Kelly
& Dr Shipman
is unfortunate
for the media

pre-emptive attack
in the offensive
double-bluff, stakes
of debate promoted
from one of comp
etence to one of
morality—looked
straight ahead, said
"look", missed the
point but continued
to talk convincing
toward the near-point
like a dad-rapper
practising in para-
rhyme

Email hours
before the last
walk—"many
dark actors
playing games"
how politics
pulls the sooty-
strings of
suicide

washing on the line: in the house style

wet handkerchief: in the house style

garden-fete: in the house style

synergy of a kettle: in the house style

july heat: in the house style

tracksuit at home: in the house style

trip to cornwall: in the house style

another question: in the house style

a long walk: in the house style

missed phonecall: in the house style

variant: *come into the woods*

still harping on about Iraq . . .

so every book is a car, then?

it has been published that George Bush is a reformed alcoholic with a conviction for drink-driving, before becoming president of the United States and the driver, publisher of the middle-east 'road map'. all aboard & welcome. belt-up in the back.

A New Iraqi Flag

"A RAT'S NEST OF RESISTANCE"
(read: we believe in our cause more than yours)
"A HOTBED OF CONTENTION"
(read: we will not sleep with fingerfucked americana)
synapse-decisions replaced with clicks
no RIPPED-UP rings on hardbacks
—one, two—blow gold from starjumps—
a flag, inevitable
in lemon kurd yellow
sliced israeli blue
with a dulux paintshop pro finish
mindshowering executives
PR men
marketeers
advertisers
"re-tuned. re-conditioned. heck, it's been
re-everythinged"
found lazy blossom
new-coke in the holy wars
man,
we shit spit over that one

A Late Arrival

eyes full of duvet
   caesarian RIPS
guilt-ground
    RIPS
ship-sized gherkin
     tailed sparks
branch
  country's cum-tree
fingertips sanding
executive tables
    bumchumming
over Kyoto
blowjobbing happy-stats
into the floss-only mouth
     of Bush

Crikey

> *"'Crikey' is a typical Blair expletive, a bit dated,
> a bit comic, designed to avoid trouble"*
> PETER STOTHARD, '30 DAYS'

crikey

chirac

christianity

crisis

High-Risk Sunday League Strategy

can we stick a bore-hole through our anomaly?
bricks & mortar up the blunderbuss waterfall?
our boring skills are much commented upon
victorian rubble not roman road runs
under goalposts—radars in punch lines—
but can we have a direct-debit guarantee
that if we RIP up the turf in measured clods
we can ever play this field again?

Some Trinkets: *for Sarah*

Some Trinkets

like H$_2$O is water
without association
you changed &
consciousness as made
of the same stuff as
rivers stones stars
which I would have
believed too that first
night

voice of the child
follows the balloon
up a staircase &
when the image
bursts tape runs
its loop there is
the little you
in green shorts
singing

fluid hieroglyph
runs between us
into us is read
again you assume
whatever space
I follow was not
wrong bow down
& into
you

then today I
have come such
a long way for you
you are always walk
ing towards me blank
ing out backlight
jealously guarding
the half-symbol of the
tongue

new letter what are
you shape I have never
seen before I dreamt
our bed outdoors
was sign language
for stars & woke
a sheetless us
clasped tight
thumbs

inexact science
of your shadow
over kitchen tiles
its length & shape
september's sun
dial in the umber
place now turn
ing in me
always

A Note for Sarah

"YES" is used so much around here.

this is important & separates us from the world.

slow black hearts of the goldfish mouths: NO NO NO.

put our bodies under the same roof by choice.

our lives together.

nose held & submerged in the bath, yr. head sways left/right.

hair follows undertowed slow as a sea-flower.

submerged, my mouth moves slow as the fish.

you haven't heard a word of this.

I have written it down for you.

Shortwood

1

key stiff in the pocket
to the front door
all the way home
to the new house.

throat like a weak apple.

no more great divide
between morning & night
shafted gear clock heart
drinking two or three nights
            & hangingover.

easy sleep ride sometime pre-alarm.

crisp fresh core.

lubricated.

2

ALL my body knows of the day
is your body

: thought this happy.

sheet gauze mist whitened
rain lashed glass to wet
& flesh bump braille beds
rose to catch each one.

brain banks mirror returned expression
like a turn of 20th century
child's face   blank
staring into the blacklens box
having never seen a film.

Slices
after Robert Creeley

you are woken
from a dream
by a ringing
phone, you
answer
& wonder
what space
you occupy

∽

yes?

yes love?

I thought you said something?

what's that?

I said I thought you said something?

no.

o.

∽

dreaming I was
just about to make
love to you
you wake me up
asking
"were you asleep?".

∽

the simple
extravagance
of more
than once.

yes.

come again.

The Girl Who Cried Fox

bunny/fox: it wouldn't be long until we played that game again.
2 o'clock — to be as near to exact as possible — in the pitch black.

bunny/fox: its beauty forgot its deconstruction.
which reminds me, that was the night you danced your dance
                               of dialectical materialism
cupped-hands to onion out the contradiction between thesis
                                     & antithesis
to meet & contradict again at synthesis
to meet & onion out again to a triumphant grip.
history of the world's hitherto existing order
danced to the theme tune of 'graham norton'.

sexy marxist.

I was in the shower, could hear your songs in my name
through the door of each drop
then an urgency, a flame to your voice. hot gone cold.

fox, fox, there's a fox in the garden.

rush to the back window wet & unclothed —
                 the raw nerve of me —
for the moment uncaring about being watched
watching the fox who doesn't care either way,
who mutates in the first seconds from dog to fox
                         to stay as fox & shock
threading its needle & red cotton
through the long, dusk-bitten grass.
sewing in tonight.

A Christmas Poem

nothing is found, only connective
20 economy images strung
into "a christmas poem"
not baubled like Betjeman's
the blue balloon's slow fish motion
rises, jaws against the skyscraper
maintained to a child's throat-note, discordant
below the wind
bookseller's paperbacks flap open/shut
like the insides of a spaghetti western piano
kinetic & unpurchasable
red milk bottle caps melt against the trains, approaching
terraces pulse ennui   decorated
all the way to the vanishing point I'm heading for
blistering strobe-like—
it's the synaesthetic taste of lights I like
explainable backwards as much
as, say, the role of ants in capitalism
an ecosystem of its own—
her shape swells & double-unlocks rouge flesh
nothing found only connective
between us such seasons take place as coincidence

Fairy Tale: The Wolf & the Book
after the French Surrealists

wake film eyed
fingers run
our names
in wet paint
down separate
childhood walls
in red blue
green sponge
house sun
field gate
outlined in
the crossed
window I
am writing
this & you
have stopped
halfway down
the path to
add some
purple extras
to the grass—

hurry love!

when the
wolf knocks
this will be
complete &
we'll be open
on this page
reflected in
our bedroom
mirror through
a hole into a
neighbour's

room huddled
in the delicate
architecture of
their imagination
as they read
unbidden but
fortunate for us

it will be warm
but open to
the elements
until the wolf
goes away or
our neighbour
reads 'the wolf
shooter' — my
next poem —
& makes the
connective
leap

Uttoxeter

in camera
it came in
        4:15 winner unbacked
rash september
            alcoholic
best-intentioned by day / undrying
stripped down walls
clouded-coils   dog-eared leaves
umber-orange skeins of faded papers
sun shot shakes on the day's unshaven lip
                then down in one

tepid between sweat & excitement
alluring/sealed off
            in black pvc
dry sun mirrored oval on thighs
smooth with finger-brakes

new original still
when arachnophobia imploded
to pub-yard brawl between spider & finger
jealous it could be everywhere
with a lens on each leg

new original still
on the outside-inside of me
like a porch on a house
wickered with light through trees

& then moving in in each other

        we turn (

hare's ground moves under us

        brown rush hones in to sinew's fretboard

    momentous hush of horse

Delicious

endless bibliography of expressions
typical of me to say   true
symposium of nuance
where we meet
lymph-nodes
jouissance resurfaces in your features
sea's surround sound through trees
from above, semaphore of yes
your beauty half-dressed
in a t-shirt
called "THE WORLD'S END"

Printed in the United Kingdom
by Lightning Source UK Ltd.
109209UKS00001B/51